essentials

essentials liefern aktuelles Wissen in konzentrierter Form. Die Essenz dessen, worauf es als „State-of-the-Art" in der gegenwärtigen Fachdiskussion oder in der Praxis ankommt. *essentials* informieren schnell, unkompliziert und verständlich

- als Einführung in ein aktuelles Thema aus Ihrem Fachgebiet
- als Einstieg in ein für Sie noch unbekanntes Themenfeld
- als Einblick, um zum Thema mitreden zu können

Die Bücher in elektronischer und gedruckter Form bringen das Fachwissen von Springerautor*innen kompakt zur Darstellung. Sie sind besonders für die Nutzung als eBook auf Tablet-PCs, eBook-Readern und Smartphones geeignet. *essentials* sind Wissensbausteine aus den Wirtschafts-, Sozial- und Geisteswissenschaften, aus Technik und Naturwissenschaften sowie aus Medizin, Psychologie und Gesundheitsberufen. Von renommierten Autor*innen aller Springer-Verlagsmarken.

Andrea Hausmann • Sarah Schuhbauer

Basic Guide to Cultural Tourism Marketing

Practice Cultural Management

 Springer

Andrea Hausmann
Institute for Cultural Management
Ludwigsburg University of Education
Ludwigsburg, Germany

Sarah Schuhbauer
Institute for Cultural Management
Ludwigsburg University of Education
Ludwigsburg, Germany

ISSN 2197-6708   ISSN 2197-6716 (electronic)
essentials
ISBN 978-3-658-39973-3   ISBN 978-3-658-39974-0 (eBook)
https://doi.org/10.1007/978-3-658-39974-0

This Springer VS imprint is published by the registered company Springer Fachmedien Wiesbaden GmbH, part of Springer Nature.
The registered company address is: Abraham-Lincoln-Str. 46, 65189 Wiesbaden, Germany

Contents

Introduction to Cultural Tourism Marketing

1.1   Concepts and characteristics

Cultural tourism is a form of tourism that refers to the (intangible or tangible) cultural heritage and/or cultural institutions, events, projects etc. of a destination. Through cultural tourism, these cultural assets of a destination are transformed into products that can be consumed by out-of-town/non-resident guests (DuCros & McKercher, 2020). These guests either come as part of a day trip/business trip or they stay overnight (in commercial accommodation, with friends, relatives etc.). What they have in common is that their main or a secondary motive is to take advantage of the cultural heritage or offer of a destination (DuCros & McKercher, 2020; Hausmann, 2019a). The right marketing plays a central role in this, because appropriate marketing measures make the cultural offer easier to use and consume for these visitors.

Marketing is generally concerned with the initiation and maintenance of *exchange relationships* in relevant markets. In this sense, marketing is always successful when all stakeholders involved in the exchange – on the supply *and* the demand side – achieve an added value or benefit: While, for example, cultural tourists experience an unforgettable afternoon at the international art exhibition *La Biennale di Venezia* in Italy, a large number of Italian and international cultural tourism service providers benefit in return, e.g. through revenues from ticket sales, city tax, transport, accommodation, restaurant visits, guided tours etc. The term *service providers* covers the very different, public and private players in the market for cultural tourism such as cultural institutions, tourism organisations, hotels, restaurants, city guides etc. (Hausmann, 2019a; Kolb, 2017; Kotler et al., 2017).

© The Author(s), under exclusive license to Springer Fachmedien
Wiesbaden GmbH, part of Springer Nature 2023
A. Hausmann, S. Schuhbauer, *Basic Guide to Cultural Tourism Marketing*,
essentials, https://doi.org/10.1007/978-3-658-39974-0_1

A basic prerequisite for an exchange to take place between the demand and supply side is that cultural tourism service providers make appropriate efforts to develop and market an offer that is attractive from the user's point of view. In this context, the understanding of marketing in this book includes both an *external, market-related* and an *internal, organization-related* perspective:

Marketing is understood to be a leadership principle and cross-functional mindset among cultural tourism service providers. The aim of cultural tourism marketing is to shape external, market-related activities and internal, organisational conditions in such a way that.

- competitive advantages are created,
- customer benefits are generated and
- organisational goals are achieved.

From this definition, characteristic *features* and *principles* of cultural tourism marketing can be derived as follows:

1. *Marketing as leadership principle and cross-functional mindset:* Marketing is not just one functional area among others and is not limited to one job/department in a touristic organisation. Even if the specific actions are planned and implemented within the framework of a particular job or the marketing department, there should be a basic cross-functional understanding of the impact of marketing. All departments should be aware that marketing – specifically the creation of competitive advantages and customer benefits – as a *guiding principle* affects all organisational areas and determines all actions in relation to the cultural tourism market. In this sense, marketing should always have a high priority, especially also at the top hierarchical level (e.g. management) of a tourism service provider.
2. *External, market related activities:* Marketing encompasses a variety of measures designed to reach the external stakeholders of cultural tourism service providers. These stakeholders include above all tourists, but also, for example, cooperation partners, local politics/cultural policy and the media. In detail, the external, market-related activities consist of analysis (environment, competition, resources, etc.), planning (goals, strategies), implementation (design of offers, pricing, etc.) and evaluation (satisfaction surveys, sales statistics etc.).
3. *Internal, organisational conditions:* On the one hand, marketing is a functional area among others to which corresponding resources (budget, staff, action com-

petences etc.) must be allocated. On the other hand, marketing is an internal mindset. This means for example that a corresponding organisational culture with a focus on customer and service orientation must be created.

4. *Creation of competitive advantages:* All cultural tourism service providers operate in a highly competitive market. To be successful here, the focus of marketing must be on creating "better" or "more attractive" offers from the perspective of potential demand (Coccossis, 2010). The aim of cultural tourism marketing is therefore to ensure that a particular touristic offer is perceived and evaluated as preferable to other touristic offers that are *subjectively* seen as alternatives by the demand side. If an offer succeeds in this, it has a *competitive advantage* (Kozak & Baloglu, 2011). The following types can be distinguished for cultural tourism service providers (Hausmann, 2021; Meffert et al., 2018; West et al., 2015):

– *Differentiation:* The competitive advantage here lies, for example, in the fact that

- a cultural tourism service provider or its offers are of better or higher quality than those of the competition (*quality*),
- they are more *innovative*, e.g. through the use of digital applications,
- they are marked, i.e. enable the advantages typically associated with a brand, e.g. emotional or symbolic advantages (*branding*) and/or
- the service orientation or customer contact is particularly good (*customer relationship*).

– *Cost:* This competitive advantage is reflected in lower costs for cultural tourists. These can be direct financial advantages (e.g. combined tickets for several museums, free parking spaces, hotel specials, free public transport) or indirect financial advantages (e.g. easy access to the destination, no traffic jams due to good road conditions, no loss of time due to good wayfinding systems).

– *Time:* This category refers, for example, to the duration of the service provision or the speed of response to booking requests. Cultural tourism service providers that offer solutions for cultural tourists faster than others usually gain a competitive advantage.

– *Reliability:* This advantage is about a service provider being more likely than its competitors to deliver on its value proposition (both in terms of basic or core functions of a service and optional additional services). Examples may be that reserved tickets are available at the box office or that rooms can be taken at the agreed time.

5. *Customer benefits:* Customer benefit is achieved through consistent customer orientation and represents the most important lever for creating competitive advantages. After all, it is the customers who decide whether they achieve a significant benefit through the exchange relationship with a tourism service provider. This is also the reason for the difference between a so-called *Unique Selling Proposition (USP)* and a competitive advantage: The USP aims to position a service on the basis of a distinguishing feature or a unique benefit. A USP is therefore initially only a *potential* competitive advantage claimed by the provider. The decisive factor is how potential target groups (e.g. young tourists or group tourists) see this offer and whether they actually recognise the claimed special features as such.

6. *Organisational goals:* The planning, selection and implementation of concrete marketing measures ties up scarce resources. Cultural tourism marketing is therefore not an end in itself, but should contribute to achieving the overarching organisational goals of a cultural tourism service provider (e.g. profit, turnover, market share, customer loyalty/satisfaction, but in the case of cultural institutions also e.g. cultural policy goals).

It should be noted that in the English-speaking world, other terms are used for this topic besides "cultural tourism". One example is the term "heritage tourism", which is also occasionally used in the literature. A closer look reveals that the terms are not clearly distinguishable. The authors of this essential understand "cultural tourism" or "cultural tourism marketing" as the broader concept/the more comprehensive term. This is because while "heritage tourism", for example, is more concerned with the places visited and their specific resources (e.g. a monument steeped in history, a landmark etc.), "cultural tourism" also encompasses local traditions and includes exhibitions in museums, festivals, concerts, etc. in its considerations.

1.2   The marketing management process

The marketing management process or marketing planning is a tool for visualising and structuring the marketing activities of cultural tourism service providers. The process can refer both to the marketing of a cultural tourism service provider as a whole (e.g. cultural institution, destination) and to the marketing of individual offers or touristic packages. In the general marketing literature, different variants of this process can be found which differ in detail with regard to the designation of the individual phases and included activities (e.g. Homburg, 2017; Kotler et al., 2017; Meffert et al., 2018). By and large, however, these variants cover similar content. For the purposes of this book, a practice-oriented, simplified process is used, which is divided into four compact phases whose activities consist of different focal points:

1. *Information phase*: Here, the analysis of the external stakeholders relevant to a tourism service provider (competitors, cooperation partners, tourists etc.) and of the internal situation (resources: budget, staff, competences; organisational structure/culture etc.) takes place. Typical tools are environmental and competition analysis, resource analysis and demand analysis. The information obtained with these methods forms the *basis* for decisions in the subsequent phases.
2. *Strategic phase*: In this phase, the (qualitative and quantitative) *goals* to be achieved by the marketing measures are first defined. Based on this, the basic *strategic direction* (e.g. with regard to branding, innovation, target groups or tourist segments to be reached or future cooperation behaviour) is determined. These decisions create a *framework for action* that is valid in the longer term and provides a binding basis for the selection of concrete marketing measures that will be implemented in the next phase.
3. *Operational phase*: The focus is here on the target- and strategy-oriented selection of concrete measures or *instruments* from the marketing mix (and thus the answer to the question of which touristic products/services are to be created, offered and promoted at what prices and via which distribution channels) and their implementation in practice.
4. *Coordination/Evaluation phase*: On the one hand, this phase includes the *coordination* of all tourism marketing activities by creating the appropriate organisational framework conditions, such as the provision of necessary resources and the connection to other organisational areas (e.g. with similar tasks). On the other hand, this phase also includes the review of the effectiveness of the marketing measures implemented or the *control* of their contribution to the achievement of the previously defined goals. The results obtained here are part of a *feedback process* and thus flow into the information-related phase of the next marketing planning process.

To conclude this section, the following should be pointed out: On the one hand, only selected marketing activities can be dealt with in more detail in the context of this *essential* (for more detailed information on the phases in culture and tourism marketing see e.g. DuCros & McKercher, 2020; Hausmann, 2019a, 2021). On the other hand, the planning process is to be understood as ideal-typical, since in tourism practice activities from different phases usually run in parallel or activities from a preceding or subsequent phase have to be taken up again or brought forward. Nevertheless, the particular strength of the planning process lies in the fact that it clearly shows what is often neglected in the day-to-day practice of cultural institutions and other tourism service providers: cultural tourism marketing basically has two different levels which, although closely interwoven, must be considered both:

- a strategic-conceptual, longer-term one and
- an operational-instrumental, short-term one.

Keeping these two levels apart in day-to-day business and pausing regularly to make operational decisions based on strategic considerations can help tourism service providers operate more successfully and sustainably in the market.

Strategic decisions in Cultural Tourism Marketing

2

2.1 Setting marketing objectives

Goals give *orientation* and enable the *evaluation* of cultural tourism marketing activities. They contain statements about desired conditions to be achieved by tourism service provider with suitable marketing strategies and measures, and thus *support* the decision-making for the use of scarce resources. It makes sense for cultural tourism organisations to systematise the development of their objectives through of a step-by-step approach (for details see Byrnes, 2009; Kotler et al., 2017; Hausmann, 2021):

- At the top level of the hierarchy of objectives is the *overall organizational purpose* (business mission) of a tourism service provider, which is determined either by the interests of private owners or by cultural, tourism or economic policy. Because the organisational purpose is typically only defined in general terms (cf. Table 2.1), it can only provide a rough orientation for operational tourism marketing.
- At the middle level of the goal hierarchy are the *functional objectives* of cultural tourism service providers (e.g. marketing goals).
- At the bottom level concrete *action objectives* are formulated which relate to individual business areas (e.g. cultural tourism in a specific region or for specific target groups) and concrete instruments from the marketing mix (e.g. social media as part of communication policy).

Table 2.1 Target hierarchy of a tourism organisation – Example: Visit Britain/Visit England

Purpose of the tourism organisation (VisitBritain/ Visit England, 2021a)	"As the national tourism agency – a non-departmental public body funded by the Department for Digital, Culture, Media & Sports (DCMS), VisitBritain/VisitEngland plays a unique role in building England's tourism product, raising Britain's profile worldwide, increasing the volume and value of tourism exports and developing England and Britain's visitor economy"
Marketing objectives (VisitBritain/ Visit England, 2021b)	– To make tourism one of the most successful and productive sectors for the UK economy – To enable Britain's tourism industry to capture its share of global and domestic growth – Adopting an agile and innovative approach – Support productivity optimisation – Be the expert body on growing tourism – Deliver a clear strategy for England – To attract 49 million visits by 2025 spending £35 billion. – Grow the value of tourism – Drive the dispersal of tourism value across Britain

As Table 2.1 further shows, marketing objectives can be *quantitative* and *qualitative* in nature: While the first category contains economic variables that can be easily collected or directly measured (e.g. booking figures, number of overnight stays, tickets sold), qualitative objectives can only be collected indirectly (e.g. through satisfaction surveys of cultural tourists or other stakeholders).

A typical problem in tourism practice is that the formulation of objectives often remains vague; this not only complicates the use of objectives to manage/control activities and resources but also the verification of their achievement. It may therefore be useful to set objectives in accordance with the *SMART principle*, i.e. a goal must meet the following requirements:

- An objective is clearly and unambiguously formulated ("<u>s</u>pecific"),
- "<u>m</u>easurable" following the implementation of a marketing measure,
- actually "<u>a</u>chievable" through appropriate marketing measures,
- important ("<u>r</u>elevant") for a cultural tourism service provider in terms of achieving the overall organisational purpose and
- has a clear "<u>t</u>ime-bound" character.

2.2 Choosing marketing strategies

Strategies are long-term behavioural plans that build on the previously defined goals and form the framework for action to achieve these goals. Strategies also serve as a binding basis for the selection of concrete measures. They are thus the *link* between marketing objectives on the one hand and the marketing mix on the other. In the general marketing literature, there are various approaches to systematising strategies (e.g. Kotler et al., 2017). A practice-oriented structuring of relevant marketing strategies results from decisions of a cultural tourism service provider in the following areas:

- which *submarkets* of the overall market for cultural tourism (e.g. in terms of regions, types of demand) are to be addressed with which service and products – i.e. with which problem-solving competence,
- which *competitive advantages* are to be created (e.g. quality, brand, innovation, costs) and
- how to behave towards other *market participants*, such as, for example, tourists, suppliers, media, communities (e.g. cooperation, relationship marketing).

The following sections focus on those strategies that traditionally play a particularly important role in the practice of cultural tourism marketing. This includes dealing with relevant types of demand (segmentation), suitable opportunities for differentiation from the competition (brand management and innovation) and behaviour towards the competition (cooperation).

2.2.1 Market Segmentation and Cultural Tourists Typology

Market segmentation is the *criteria-based* division of a *heterogeneous* market into market segments that are *homogeneous* in terms of their reaction to certain marketing measures. The *gaols* of market segmentation are

- to better address the different needs and expectations of different touristic target groups,
- thereby making it easier to attract and satisfy them (and, if possible, to retain them),
- to possibly generate higher revenues and
- to build or maintain competitive advantages.

In summary, the aim is to achieve a greater congruence between touristic supply and demand than if the market as a whole is treated in an undifferentiated manner. Typical criteria that are suitable for segmenting the cultural tourism market are:

- *Socio-demographic* and *geographical* criteria, such as age, education, occupation, nationality, number of kids, income, and place of residence of cultural tourists.
- *Psychographic* criteria, such as the degree of interest in culture (e.g. culture as a lifestyle in everyday life or only when travelling) or the general attitude towards culture.
- *Behaviour- and benefit-oriented* criteria, such as the importance of culture as a reason for visiting or as a motive to travel (primary or secondary motive), type of prior knowledge (e.g. experts in a particular field vs. laypersons), guest status (e.g. day/overnight visitors, group/individual travellers, domestic/foreign guests), brand loyalty (e.g. regular vs. first-time visitors), perceived benefits (e.g. education, edutainment, individual or package services), perceived quality (for core services, but also for use of complementary services, e.g. in the cafeteria of a heritage site), information and media usage behaviour (online, offline etc.) and price behaviour (e.g. maximum willingness to pay).

Of particular importance for the typologisation of demand in cultural tourism are the criteria "importance of culture as a reason for travel" (e.g. DuCros & McKercher, 2020; Richards 2003), "guest status" (e.g. DTV, 2006; Pröbstle 2016) and "type of prior knowledge" (e.g. TMBW, 2011). In cultural touristic analyses and marketing concepts, they often form the first level of segmentation before additional criteria are included at further levels in order to be able to describe/delimit the target groups as concretely as possible by combining several criteria.

Target Group: Preferred Target Groups for the Icelandic Tourism Industry
"(…) the preferred target groups for the Icelandic tourism industry: The Fun-loving Globetrotter, the Independent Explorer and the Cultural Comfort Seeker. The target groups have been analysed depending on their lifestyle, personality and how they meet the needs and goals of Icelandic tourism. These are mostly travellers with higher salaries, that travel at least once per year and are always searching for new experiences and destinations, they want to connect to the local culture and respect the environment. Although they are different in many ways, they can be defined by the experiences they search for and their lifestyles" (Promote Iceland, 2017, p.7).

Table 2.2 Segments and segment-specific marketing measures

Segment	Purposeful cultural tourists	Occasional cultural tourists	Incidental cultural tourists
Key features of target group	Culture is the main reason for a trip, usually several cultural institutions are visited	Culture is not the main reason for travelling, rather several vacation activities (hiking, shopping etc.) are combined	The use of culture is random, e.g. because originally planned holiday activities are cancelled due to weather conditions
Key aspects of cultural tourism marketing	– Exquisite, complex service bundles with partners from the same and/or different stages of the tourism value chain – Thematic bracket for the products linked in the tourism service chain – Focus on knowledge acquisition, education and the "special moment" – Focus on brand management and high-quality management – Premium price for unique offers (e.g. "meet the curator") – High-quality, supra-regional communication measures, special distribution channels	– Offerings focused on edutainment and usability – Enabling quick "snapshots"/rather superficial experiences; focus on cultural "must sees" – Price differentiation (especially combined tickets/discounts) – Good presence/ visibility of the cultural/touristic site (e.g. museum flags) – Good wayfinding system at the destination – Focus on local/ regional communication and distribution	– Good presence/ visibility of the cultural/touristic site (e.g. museum flags) – Good wayfinding system at the destination – Accessibility of a site ("openness" of the entrance area, friendly service staff etc.) – Products with a focus on edutainment, usability, and easy consumption – Price differentiation (discounts etc.) – Local/regional communication and distribution

The particular characteristics of different submarkets or target groups thus always form the starting point for deriving specific marketing measures, e.g. in the context of designing the offer (duration, time of day, required prior knowledge etc.), pricing (premium prices, discounts etc.) or designing communication measures (communication channels, breadth/depth of information etc.). Table 2.2 uses a simple target group model to illustrate how target group-specific marketing priorities can be set through the formation of different segments (for more details see also DuCros & McKercher, 2020).

It is easy to understand that such a segment-specific approach is resource-intensive. This is particularly relevant for cultural and heritage sites with scarce resources and smaller tourism service providers outside urban centres. A segment-specific approach should therefore be based on the following criteria (see also DuCros & McKercher, 2020; Hausmann, 2021):

* *Relevance to purchasing behaviour:* The segmentation criteria used (e.g. age, place of residence) are a prerequisite for the use of a particular cultural tourism offer.
* *Accessibility:* The target groups identified by means of segmentation criteria (e.g. day tourists) can be specifically addressed with specific measures.
* *Economic efficiency:* The benefits resulting from segmentation and differentiated targeting (e.g. income from day tourism) are greater than the costs incurred by the development of segment-specific marketing measures (e.g. costs for advertising in neighbouring regions, multilingual website/social media activities).
* *Durability:* the segments formed are stable over a longer-term planning period.

2.2.2 Brands and branding

Another strategic option for creating competitive advantages is to build and maintain brands. Empirical studies show that this is also a virulent topic in cultural tourism. In the interaction between culture and tourism there is always an urgent need for action to ensure that tourism organisations and cultural venues agree on a common understanding for profiling a destination (Burzinski et al., 2018). To achieve this, a brand with a strong identity must be built (e.g. Aaker, 1996; Keller, 1993).

Brands are first of all names, signs, symbols etc. or a combination of them to identify the products and services of tourism providers, such as cultural institutions, heritage sites, tour operators, and to distinguish them from their competitors. Furthermore, strong brands create *images* in the minds of the relevant stakeholders (here: cultural tourists) that influence their selection behaviour in a competitive environment (Esch, 2014). A strong brand represents a kind of "personality" with a clearly recognisable, distinguishable character; it stands for competence and the keeping of promises. In terms of tourism demand, strong brands have the following *functions* (DuCros & McKercher, 2020; Kolb, 2017):

* Brands can communicate the benefits of a product, a trip, a visit quickly and easily. In this way, brands serve as a *signpost* for cultural tourists and help them select cultural tourism service providers as they enable faster information absorption and processing.

* Brands *signal* a certain, expectable service quality and thus help to reduce quality uncertainty and the perceived purchase risk for cultural tourists.
* Brands offer *additional emotional stimuli* (experience/image/prestige value); they enable cultural tourists to identify and express themselves with the brand of a product, site or destination (individuality, group membership, social status etc.).

Branding or brand management includes all measures to build and develop a brand. These are taken with the aim of making a cultural tourism offer stand out from a wide range of similar offers. In addition, this should make it possible to clearly assign partial services to a specific brand. *Identity-based* brand management is particularly suitable for this purpose by integrating an *outside-in perspective* (i.e. demand or image orientation) and an *inside-out perspective* (employee and competence orientation). The aim is thus to align

* the *self-image* of a tourism service provider (brand *identity*) with
* the *external image* of tourism demand (brand *image*) (Burmann et al., 2017).

The most important activities of brand management include:

1. *Brand positioning:* Here, the aim is to make decisions on how to anchor one's own brand in the perception of cultural tourism demand as clear and unmistakable as possible compared to competing touristic brands (Table 2.3). The more

Table 2.3 Dimensions of brand positioning in cultural tourism

Dimension	Questions	Explanation
Brand competence	Who is the brand?	Central brand assets: Brand history, origin of the brand, significance of the brand in the tourism market, touristic infrastructure, service orientation etc
Brand image	How does the brand appear?	Perceptible/audible impression: Word/picture mark, shape/pattern mark, verbal/sound mark, combined mark
Brand benefits	What does the brand offer?	Value propositions, functional and emotional benefits: Attractive touristic packages, value for money, quality of service, accessibility, cultural/regional specifics etc
Brand personality/ properties	How is the brand?	Emotions connected to the brand: Authentic, versatile, honest, fancy, traditional, sympathetic, colourful, reliable, exclusive, down-to-earth, natural etc

unique a brand's positioning is the less interchangeable the marked products and services are from the point of view of cultural tourists.

2. *Brand architecture*: The brand architecture informs about the arrangement of different touristic brands, especially about the roles of the individual brands and their relationships to each other. The following strategic options are available:

   – *Individual or product brand strategy*: Each product of a service provider (e.g. destination) is offered under its *own* brand; the superordinate brand fades into the background. This strategy is suitable if the individual brands are very strong and/or very differently positioned.

   – *Umbrella brand strategy*: Here, the services are offered under *one* brand. The umbrella brand represents the superordinate brand in the brand system which combines the individual or product brands under one name. The umbrella brand does usually not advertise its own services but refers to the individual or product brands. As Table 2.4 shows, umbrella brands can be found among service providers from both the cultural and tourism sector.

2.2.3   Innovation

Another way to stand out from competition is through innovation. In tourism, *digitisation* and the use of information and communication technologies (ICTs) play a major role in this respect:

> "In recent years, digitalization has drastically transformed the tourism sector, revolutionizing the way we travel and along with it almost every aspect of doing business. The increased use of social media, big data, artificial intelligence and predictive analytics provide powerful tools for improving the quality of the sector through greater accuracy, strategic insight and better engagement with the traveler" (UNWTO, 2019a).

Accordingly, the digitisation strategy and the digital skills of a tourism service provider aim at building competitive advantages with the help of ICTs, which are also perceived and assessed as such by the (potential) demand. The chosen digitisation strategy then triggers activities in all areas of the marketing mix in the operational implementation.

ICT is a generic term for all hardware and software used to store, process and exchange information. ICTs that are particularly important for cultural tourism marketing include (mobile) websites, social media (such as Facebook and Instagram), (mobile) apps, QR codes, multimedia stations, virtual tours and aug-

Table 2.4 Brand architectures in cultural tourism

Dresden State Art Collections	Visit Estonia
Umbrella brand	Umbrella brand
Under the umbrella brand *Dresden State Art Collections* 15 independent museums and four cultural institutions are brought together to form one of the oldest, largest, and most important museum networks in the world. In 2018 a new word/picture brand was created with the aim of creating a visual bracket for the association (SKD, 2019).	The umbrella brand *Visit Estonia* stands as a connecting bracket for Estonia as a tourist destination with its tourist regions and service providers. The umbrella brand refers to three individual or product brands, each with a different orientation for holidays in Estonia. The individual or product brands pick up on people's preferences and showcase the country's special strengths (Visit Estonia, 2020)
Individual or product brands	Individual or product brands
1. Royal Palace (green vault, coin cabinet, cabinet of prints, drawings and photographs, armoury) 2. Zwinger with semper building (old masters picture gallery, porcelain collection, Royal Cabinet of mathematical and physical instruments, sculpture collection) 3. Albertinum (sculpture collection) 4. Art gallery in the Lipsius building (art exhibitions of contemporary painters) 5. Jägerhof (Saxon folk art Museum with puppet theatre collection) 6. Japanese palace (Museum of Ethnology Dresden; archive of the Avant-Garde) 7. Pillnitz Castle (Museum of Decorative Arts) 8. GRASSI ethnographical museum Leipzig 9. Ethnological museum Herrnhut 10. Josef Hegenbarth archive	1. *Experience with nature*: Stands for nature-based, passion-led experiences; audience: Natural nomads, with a strong desire to connect more with nature, to learn about new environments and experience new adventures 2. *Experience with culture*: The focus is on culture-based passion-led experiences; audience: Culture scouts, with a desire to develop their understanding of local life through historical site visits and cultural activities and with different approaches to travel, "from busy professionals in search of a fast culture fix, to those with the time to explore a nation's roots – And their own" 3. *Experience with food*: Refers to food-based passion-led experiences; audience: Flavour seekers which are driven by a desire to uncover and experience local ingredients, flavours and dishes

mented reality (Hausmann & Weuster, 2017; Law et al., 2014). These examples exemplify how different ICTs can be in terms of their technical requirements, their focus of application, their possibilities for interaction and participation etc. The following categories have emerged from research activities of the authors. However, due to the broad range of applications of most ICTs and their connectivity with each other, these categories cannot be without overlap (Hausmann, 2018; Hausmann & Schuhbauer, 2020):

- ICTs with a focus on *information gathering*, i.e. ICTs used by cultural tourists primarily to obtain information about the offerings, service, and quality features etc. of the tourism providers in general and cultural attractions/heritage sites in specific; this includes basic services such as online registration (e.g. guided tours) or online booking (e.g. tickets).
- ICTs with a focus on *interaction* with cultural tourism service providers and/or third parties (especially other cultural tourists), which are primarily used by the demand side to establish personal contact with the service providers and/or to exchange service and quality experiences with others. The most frequently used instruments in this category include travel portals, Facebook, YouTube and Instagram; Twitter, on the other hand, has no noteworthy significance in cultural tourism.
- ICTs with a focus on the *location-independent, virtual use* of objects. This includes applications that are primarily used by cultural tourism demand to deal with what is to be seen on site regardless of a service provider's opening hours, location etc., often in preparation for a later "real" visit (e.g. online collections, virtual tours, panoramic pictures).
- ICTs with a focus on the *location-bound, individual experience enrichment* of the visit, i.e. ICTs used by cultural tourists to draw on additional, more detailed and/or multimedia-based information during the visit and to enhance the quality of the experience on site (e.g. multimedia stations, audio guides, augmented reality, apps, QR codes, virtual worlds).

However, as the Cultural Tourism Study 2018, a large online survey with 606 cultural tourism providers in Germany, empirically proves, the service providers in the market for cultural tourism still lag far behind the general trend (Burzinski et al., 2018). For example, in product policy or specifically for services in the area of education/audience development which is important for cultural tourism, it is apparent that cultural institutions have so far relied primarily on traditional "offline" formats rather than on those that use new, digital approaches to enable

Table 2.5 Formats of mediation (multiple answers; Burzinski et al., 2018, p. 14)

Traditional formats	Digital formats
– Overview tours (77,9%) – Themed tours (e.g. period, person) (71.7%) – Special tours (e.g. "at night in the museum") (54.0%) – Workshops (45,3%) – Audio guides (34,4%)	– Join-in/multi-media stations (29.3%) – Apps/QR codes (18.1%)

edutainment and experimentation (Table 2.5); the situation is similar in distribution and communication policy (Sects. 3.4 and 3.5). A study by Schuhbauer/Hausmann (2021) shows that three years later not much has changed, especially in rural areas. While German tourism organisations and municipal cultural administrations are already using ICTs quite actively, cultural institutions in particular are still very hesitant (for further reasons see Sect. 3.5).

As research at the *Institute for Cultural Management* of the Ludwigsburg University of Education shows, this is all the more regrettable as ICTs offer cultural tourism a wide range of marketing potential in all three phases of the *customer journey* (Hausmann, 2019b; Hausmann & Schuhbauer, 2020). The ranking in Table 2.6 is based on the assumed importance of a category in the respective travel phase and is to be understood as exemplary, as it always depends on the concrete characteristics of a user (e.g. age, place of residence, previous experience).

In view of the great potential that has been little used in cultural tourism marketing so far, it is at least encouraging that cultural institutions are aware of their deficits. Well over two thirds (73%) of the cultural institutions included in the above mentioned online study agree with the following statement: "The maintenance of internet platforms and social networks is absolutely necessary to adequately serve the information needs of visitors" (Burzinski et al., 2018, p.38; translation by the authors). The fact that the cultural institutions not yet reached this point is primar-

Table 2.6 ICTs in the context of the customer journey

Phase	Online focus on demand side activities	Types of ICTs used
Before the tourist's journey	Search for information, estimation/agreement, planning, reservation, booking or purchase	ICTs for information gathering; ICTs for interaction with cultural tourism service providers and/or third parties; ICTs for location-independent, virtual use of objects
During the tourist's journey	Orientation on site, searching for detailed information, (re)planning activities, using the services offered, sharing experiences with others, contacting service providers	ICTs for information gathering; ICTs for localised, individual experience enrichment of the visit; ICTs for interaction with cultural tourism service providers and/or third parties
After the tourist's journey	Share experiences with others, contact the service provider, follow up on the travel or visit experience	ICTs for interaction with cultural tourism service providers and/or third parties; ICTs for location-independent, virtual use of objects; ICTs for information gathering

ily due to poor organisational framework conditions. One in two of the respondents (55.1%) states in this regard: "We would like to make much greater use of the digital possibilities but we lack staff and know-how" (Burzinski et al., 2018, p. 38; translation by the authors). Similar results regarding the basic willingness and the lack of opportunities were reached by an interview study with practitioners in cultural heritage/tourism management conducted by the *Institute for Cultural Management* at the PH Ludwigsburg (Hausmann & Weuster, 2017).

Nevertheless, the availability of resources is only one of several necessary prerequisites for a successful digitisation strategy. Further prerequisites are:

- *Knowledge of target groups*: ICTs are being used by an increasing number of cultural tourists as part of their day trip or travel. However, there are target group-specific differences with regard to which ICTs are used in which phase of the journey and to what extent. Above all, age plays an important role here: While older people, for example, use ICTs primarily to obtain information (e.g. website or online booking), younger people use ICTs primarily for interaction (e.g. Facebook or YouTube) or for experience enrichment of the visit (e.g. virtual worlds, QR codes or apps). The use of ICTs is also affected by whether the visitors are first-time visitors or regular visitors: People who visit cultural institutions at least once every few months use the classic ICTs (i.e.

Reasons for Using or Not Using ICT of Cultural Institutions
In a survey of visitors to the *Zollverein UNESCO World Heritage* Site, a Coal Mine Industrial Complex in the heart of Germany which is highly attractive for cultural tourists, and which already uses numerous ICTs for different stages of the customer journey, it was found that ICTs are used for a variety of *reasons* (Hausmann & Schuhbauer, 2020):

- The main uses of ICTs were to obtain information (86%), plan visits (77%) and understand cultural activities (60%).
- About half of the respondents agreed that ICTs make it possible for them to access cultural institutions at any time (54%), that they can be active themselves (50%) and communicate more easily with the institutions (49%), that ICTs make cultural activities more entertaining (48%) and that they can view rooms and objects more easily (44%).

(continued)

(continued)

– Around one in three of the respondents (36%) used ICTs to experience the cultural visit in a playful way; less than a quarter of the respondents in the sample used ICTs to share their own cultural visit with others (24%).

The same study also asked respondents who had previously indicated that they do not use ICTs provided by cultural institutions to state their reasons for this (Hausmann & Schuhbauer, 2020):

– The main arguments for non-use were the reasons that the use of other or traditional media, e.g. press or posters, is sufficient (38%), that the respondents prefer the personal exchange (37%) and/or that they show no interest in the use of ICTs (30%). And as many as one in five respondents said that they were not aware of ICTs (19%).
– On the other hand, only one in ten respondents said that they are unfamiliar with ICTs and/or think ICTs are too complicated to use (12%) or feel they provide too much information (11%).
– Also, only a clear minority does not have a mobile device or internet access (7%) and only 5% of all respondents have security concerns or concerns about the protection of data privacy.

the website, the online booking of tickets or audio guides) more often than visitors who visit cultural institutions only once a year or less (Hausmann & Schuhbauer, 2020).

- *Organisational culture*: The successful use of ICTs requires an appropriate organisational culture which must be lived "top down" by management (and answered "bottom up" by employees) (see e.g. Byrnes, 2009). On the one hand, innovative action (and thus openness or courage for change) should be promoted in the various departments of a high performer. On the other hand, a "culture of mistakes" should contribute to daring to do something new and learning from failures.
- *Organisational structure:* Municipal cultural and tourism organisations with strong hierarchical communication and decision-making structures may be less successful in implementing a digitisation strategy than those organisations that can react more flexibly to market changes. The bundling of tasks in one position is also a key success factor. This position, equipped with authority to act and a sufficient budget, can be assigned to the marketing department, if available. Alternatively, an independent department can be created to bundle all digital activities (as in Germany, for example, at the renowned historical museum *Haus*

der Geschichte der Bundesrepublik Deutschland Foundation in Bonn, with its own "Digital Services" department, or also at the *Württemberg State Museum* in Stuttgart, with its "Digital Museum practice & IT" department; at both: Status July 2022).

- *Implementation plan*: It is important to put the digitisation strategy in writing and thus bindingly define what, by who, with whom, by when and with what objective is to be implemented. It follows from such a plan that the content design of ICTs is not limited to individual jobs or departments in an organisation. For social media, for example, it is essential that information from different areas of a service provider is compiled for interesting "stories", i.e. that the organisation digitally markets itself as a complete product.
- *Priority setting*: As already mentioned above, the use of ICTs requires time, staff, material resources and money i.e. it leads to opportunity costs (i.e. alternative projects cannot be realised). In view of the large number of possible ICTs, it is therefore crucial to concentrate on those that are most important from a demand perspective. Nevertheless, many smaller players will only be able to meet the demands associated with ICTs with the help of cooperation, which is therefore examined below.

However, since the beginning of 2020, the Corona crisis has given new impetus to the debate on ICTs. In a recent study by the authors of this essential many of the cultural institutions reported that they are now more intensively exploring the possibilities of ICTs. In addition to digital exhibitions, ICTs were now also used to facilitate site visits under pandemic conditions. QR code boards and films on various platforms were used for this purpose (Schuhbauer & Hausmann, 2022). It remains to be seen to what extent these digital offers will establish themselves in

Digital Offers in Cultural Institutions Due to Covid

Below are some examples of digital offerings from different countries that were created before or during the Corona crisis:

- **Galerie Tanja Wagner, Germany:** On her gallery's website, Tanja Wagner has been presenting video works by selected artists since the beginning of the corona pandemic. At the same time, these works have been or are being promoted via social media channels such as Instagram (dw, 2020).
- **Art Basel Hong Kong, China:** In 2020, Art Basel has created a virtual platform due to the cancellation of the fair. The "Online Viewing Rooms"

(continued)

(continued)

featured 235 participating galleries and over 2000 works of art that could be viewed and purchased without any risk of infection (dw, 2020).

- **Mancomunitat de la Ribera Alta, Spain:** On the website of the Mancomunitat de la Ribera Alta, a territorial community that brings together all the municipalities in the Ribera Alta region in Spain, some only free available elements of the natural and cultural heritage of the region were included. These new virtual visits were introduced during the COVID-19 outbreak. Besides the 360 images and videos that make up the routes, the application includes some additional information. During the lockdown, when the museums were not open, three times as many online visits as normal could be counted (Interreg Europe, 2021).

- **Städel Museum, Germany:** The renowned art museum has been considered one of the absolute pioneers in the field of digital offerings long before Covid. The offers are very diverse and many of them can be used from home, independently of the visit to the museum. Examples of this are "Close up" (a closer look at the Städel's collection of contemporary art, through the use of various analogue and digital media), "Digitorial" (Digital exhibitions in preparation for the exhibition on site, with texts, audios and images), the "Digital Collection" (main research platform for the Städel Museum's entire collection) or "Art History Online – The Städel course on modern art" (to learn about art history and visual studies, based on 250 selected works from the collection) (Städel Museum, 2021).

- **Museo Galileo, Italy:** At the Museo Galileo in Italy, a free guide to the museum has been developed for smartphones and tablets. The app allows visitors to explore the museum's entire collection, not only in the museum but also from home. Visitors will find descriptions of all the exhibited objects, over four hours of videos, audio commentaries and 700 pages of biographies, definitions, and technical terms. The texts are available in both Italian and English (Museo Galileo, 2018).

- **Theaterhaus Stuttgart, Germany:** Theaterhaus Stuttgart, a private theatre in Stuttgart, in the south of Germany, created the app "DanceAR" together with xailabs GmbH in 2021. The content of the app is augmented reality premieres of the Gauthier Dance/Dance Company Theaterhaus Stuttgart ensemble. The project was funded by the Federal Government Commissioner for Culture and the Media as part of an initiative to support cultural workers in Covid times. In addition, the project received funding from the Federal State of Baden-Württemberg (Theaterhaus Stuttgart, 2021).

the cultural institutions beyond the Corona crisis and to what extent the crisis has contributed to a rethinking in the long term.

2.2.4 Cooperation and networks

Entering cooperation and building networks is considered an important strategy in marketing and is also seen as the linchpin of success in cultural tourism (DuCros & McKercher, 2020; Föhl & Pröbstle, 2013; Polese, 2010). The type and scope of cooperation can be very different; it can be

- temporary and selective (e.g. theme year),
- related to recurring events (e.g. city festival, Long Night of the Museums) or
- beyond individual events and for an unlimited period (regional passes, guest cards, founding of a tourism association etc.).

Cooperation and networks are such a popular marketing strategy in cultural tourism because they help to overcome the challenges of the typically rather small-scale provider structure, especially in rural areas, and the resulting problem of lone fighters (Drda-Kühn & Wiegand, 2010; Raich & Zehrer, 2013). Especially outside the metropolitan areas, smaller cultural attractions, heritage sites and other tourist operators are often not attractive enough to attract cultural tourists (Mendonca et al., 2018; Neumeier & Pollermann, 2014; Polo & Frias, 2010). Only through cooperation and the joint development, bundling and marketing of attractive cultural tourism packages can all service providers in the value chain benefit. In cultural tourism marketing the following *forms* of cooperation are typical:

(1) Horizontal Cooperation/Networks

This form takes place between service providers at the *same* stage of a value chain, i.e. the partners offer similar or complementary cultural tourism services (e.g. several museums in a region or different castles and palaces). Such a partnership is relatively easy to implement because the parties involved often already know each other well and/or have similar interests. As studies repeatedly show, horizontal partnerships in cultural tourism are mainly entered in order to

- facilitate an informal exchange of experience or transfer of know-how with other cultural attractions/heritage sites,
- design joint events and programmes,
- coordinate dates when planning events,

- create joint information material,
- develop and implement joint marketing campaigns,
- operate a joint online platform,
- develop or distribute combined tickets and passes and/or
- to develop or market joint travel packages (e.g. Burzinski et al., 2018; Föhl & Pröbstle, 2013; Polese, 2010; Van der Zee & Vanneste, 2015).

Further objectives of horizontal cooperation and networks in cultural tourism can be:

- expansion/supplementation of own service offer,
- creation of common quality standards and thus improvement of own service offer,
- joint financing of necessary qualification measures (e.g. service staff),
- creation of a common (cultural) brand,
- strengthening of own position towards sponsors and cultural policy and
- acquisition of funding and third-party/project funds (e.g. European Regional Development Fund – ERDF 2021–2027).

Bellinzona Pass (Switzerland)
The *Bellinzona Pass* is an entrance ticket to the *Three Castles of Bellinzona*, a UNESCO World Heritage site since 2000, and the civic museum *Villa dei Cedri*. Tickets include entrance to the castles of *Bellinzona*, entrance to museums, permanent and temporary exhibitions of the Castles and entrance to *Villa dei Cedri* (Agenzia turistica ticinese SA, 2022).

Since cultural tourists often want to take advantage of attractive tourist "packages", however, the horizontal form of cooperation quickly reaches its limits; partners from other value-added stages are usually needed to design more complex and appealing tourist products.

(2) Vertical Cooperation/Networks

In this form, service providers from *various* upstream or downstream stages of the tourism value chain work together. Such partnerships result in more complex tourism products, as the various services of the partners are bundled and offered to the customer as a package (culture plus dinner, accommodation, transport etc.). As studies show, vertical cooperation in cultural tourism practice is entered into by cultural attractions and heritage sites primarily with the following partners:

- Travel media (i.e. travel guides, tourism magazines etc.),
- accommodation sector,
- catering/food service,
- tour operators,
- transport,
- retail (Burzinski et al., 2018; DuCros & McKercher, 2020; Föhl & Pröbstle, 2013).

Further important partners for cultural attractions and heritage sites include: Tourism organisations (tourism associations, tourism marketing organisations) at the various levels (local, regional etc.), tour guides, travel agents, other players in the leisure market (e.g. wellness providers).

Holiday Region Black Forest
Guest cards are a very popular marketing instrument for vertical cooperation. With the *SchwarzwaldCard,* cultural tourists get free entry to over 200 adventure attractions in the Black Forest, a mountain region in the southwest of Germany and one of its most important tourist regions. The *Schwarzwald-Card* entitles the guests to one-time free entry to the *SchwarzwaldCard* attractions (from thermal baths and ski lifts to museums and city tours) on three days of choice within one year of the date of purchase. With the bonus partners, the cultural tourists can also visit the attractions once outside of these three days. In addition, there is also the option of the *Schwarzwald Card 365* which allows tourists to visit the attractions all year round (https://www.schwarzwald-tourismus.info/planen-buchen/schwarzwaldcard).

Vertical cooperation has a number of advantages for the partners involved. Figure 2.1 shows which individual and joint goals can be achieved through vertical cooperation.

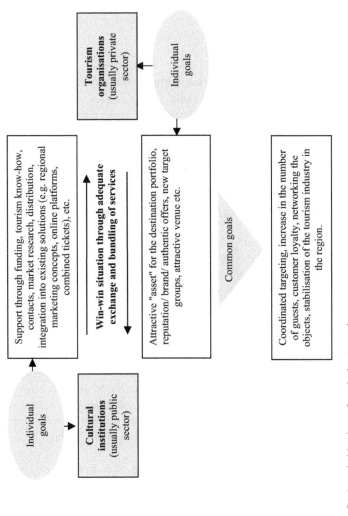

Fig. 2.1 Goals and objectives of vertical cooperation

(3) Lateral Cooperation/Networks

Finally, there is the cooperation on a lateral level, in which partners from totally different sectors work together, e.g. cultural attractions/heritage sites and companies from the insurance or banking sector. A typical form of lateral cooperation in cultural tourism is sponsoring. Sponsoring can enable the development of cultural offerings, which can then be marketed to tourists.

> **The "Digital Concert Hall" of the Berlin Philharmonic Orchestra**
> The "Digital Concert Hall" of the *Berlin Philharmonic Orchestra* was established in 2008. The *Berliner Philharmoniker* have done pioneering work with this project. With the help of the "Digital Concert Hall" classical orchestral music is to be made available worldwide beyond the venue and time of the concerts. Furthermore, the "Digital Concert Hall" serves to document the interpretations of the orchestra and its conductors. During the Covid 19 pandemic in 2020, the "Digital Concert Hall" also offered free access for 30 days. Free access is also provided to students. However, the project could only be realised through a cooperation with *Deutsche Bank*, the largest bank in Germany (https://www.digitalconcerthall.com/en). The partnership between the *Berliner Philharmoniker* and *Deutsche Bank* has now existed for 30 years. And with the help of *Deutsche Bank*, numerous other projects have also come into being (https://www.berliner-philharmoniker.de/en/titelgeschichten/20192020/deutsche-bank/).

Concluding Thoughts on Recurring Problems of Cooperation in Tourism Practice
Regarding the *functionality* of the above-mentioned partnerships, however, it is a recurring experience of many service providers that the cooperation often does not run smoothly, especially in partnerships between public and private organisations. A basic problem arises from the fact that culture and tourism seem to speak a "different language" (DuCros & McKercher, 2020; Hausmann, 2019a):

* *Cultural attractions and heritage sites* usually work in a *content-* or *supply-oriented way*. At least in Europe, they are typically publicly funded and are thus

relatively independent of (economic) market success. At the same time, they are often subject to bureaucratic procedures (e.g. hierarchical and/or political decision-making processes), which makes it difficult to react flexibly to the market. They tend to see the (artistic, content-related, scientific) core of their work threatened by cooperation with tourism professionals and are reluctant to engage in (supposedly but sometimes actual) overly bold or blaring marketing.

- *Tour operators* are *demand-driven* because they must finance themselves through the market. Their decisions are primarily economic and heavily influenced by how marketable an offer is and how it can contribute to generating growth (number of guests and overnight stays etc.) They are aware – unlike some of their public partners – that they operate in a highly competitive market. To survive in this market in the long term, they are constantly looking for ways to raise the profile of their offerings, satisfy customer needs and create competitive advantages.

If it is not possible for the partners to acknowledge their differences and find common goals, this often leads to real "struggles of faith" (Burzinski, 2016, p.14; translation by the authors). This can only be avoided if the partners engage with each other's perspectives and interests. That means specifically (for more see e.g. DuCros & McKercher, 2020):

- *Cultural institutions* must become familiar with the mechanisms and rules of the tourism market to better understand the private sector context. Early planning of events (at least one year in advance in the case of large events), professional advertising (professional multimedia marketing appropriate to target groups), networking in ticketing and the use of supra-regional ticket platforms, the provision of fixed ticket contingents for tour operators, the consideration of commission payments to travel agents when calculating prices and the primacy of service and customer orientation is expected as a matter of course by tourism operators.
- *Tourism professionals* must see cultural institutions as equal partners from the outset and negotiate with them on "eye level". They must understand the core of cultural work, be interested in the legitimate sensitivities of (public) cultural operators and take into account possible concerns. Under no circumstances should a marketing campaign be imposed against the wishes of cultural attractions/heritage sites.

Pitfalls in the Use of Cooperation
In the following, a practical example is described to illustrate the problems mentioned above. Within the framework of an interview study, various cultural tourism stakeholders of the cooperation project around the web app "The Legend of the Call of the Mountain" in the Zugspitz Region in southern Germany were interviewed – both cultural institutions and tourism organisations. Based on the interview results, four key pitfalls were identified that related to the use of cooperation for the implementation of digital applications in rural cultural tourism marketing (Schuhbauer/Hausmann, 2021). These key pitfalls were:

- Challenges in the long-term financing of cooperation projects (especially a lack of defining the responsibilities for such funding),
- destination-specific characteristics of rural areas,
- doubts about the use of evaluations and its consequences (evaluations were therefore not used in practice) and
- the limited horizon of many cultural institutions (many of them have only looked after their own needs and interests).

Recommendations for the Successful Implementation of Cooperation
In view of the different interests, working methods etc. of the public and private cultural tourism sector, in practice it is often recommended that activities be coordinated by a so-called "caretaker" who helps to ensure the long-term functionality and viability of the network. Such an intermediary role can be assumed by cultural managers, for example, who have learned to think in terms of the duality of culture and management or market. The literature on cultural tourism marketing additionally mentions a variety of conditions that must be fulfilled for a cooperation to be successful (e.g. DuCros & McKercher, 2020; Polese, 2010; Schuhbauer & Hausmann, 2021). These success criteria can be found in Table 2.7.

Table 2.7 Checklist for cooperation / networks in cultural tourism marketing

Common goals and interests
Consensual, marketable content
Concrete benefit/added value for all parties involved
(power/specialist/process) promoters; "caretakers" of the partnership and its success (coordinators)
Clarified financing of the cooperation (not only the start-up funding but also for the long-term costs); no resource bottlenecks; consideration of other funding options if necessary (e.g. donations, EU funding)
Favourable (cultural) political conditions (e.g. financial support or other commitment)
Clear structures, unambiguous allocation of responsibilities/competencies
Professional management and leadership
Transparency (decisions, funding, political interests etc.)
Clear rules, binding nature; rights and obligations set out in writing (also: Entry/exit/exclusion criteria).
Exchange of resources and competences, which ideally complement each other
Good communication, regular exchanges, institutionalised meetings
Trust; "right chemistry"; recognition of mutual strengths; meeting at "eye level", openness
Teamwork and decision-making ability of the participants
Regular evaluations of implemented measures (and of cooperation as a whole) that are custom-fit and geared to the needs of the various actors

Operational Decisions in Cultural Tourism Marketing

3

3.1 The Marketing Mix

Considering the strategic decisions discussed above, the next phase in the planning process deals with decisions regarding the operational implementation of marketing. The *instruments* available here are also referred to in the literature as the *marketing mix* or the four *"Ps"*. Given the compactness of this essential the focus in the following will be on selected aspects (in detail e.g. DuCros & McKercher, 2020; Hausmann, 2021). In order to be able to make a practice-oriented selection, guidelines have been reviewed which all refer to instruments in the areas of product, price, sales (distribution) and communication (e.g. , 2019; TMB, 2013; TMBW, 2011; Tourismus NRW, 2018).

3.2 Services

The cultural tourism offer is often made up of many individual services which, although they come from different partners in the value chain (e.g. museums, transport companies, hotels, restaurants), are regularly perceived as a complete package by the customers within the framework of their cultural tourism journeys.

> "A tourism product is a combination of tangible and intangible elements, such as natural, cultural and man-made resources, attractions, facilities, services and activities around a specific centre of interest which represents the core of the destination marketing mix and creates an overall visitor experience including emotional aspects for the potential customers" (UNWTO, 2019b, p.18).

At the same time, the specificity results from the fact that in cultural tourism services with a high proportion of immateriality predominate. In concrete terms this means that exhibitions in castles, guided tours of castles, bus transport to city festivals etc. are not tangible and thus cannot be stored or transported. As a result, the creation of the service – which also regularly requires the cooperation (e.g. watching, listening, boarding) of cultural tourists ("integration of the external factor") coincides with its use on site ("uno actu principle"). This also means that the quality of cultural tourism services cannot typically be checked in advance of their use by those requesting them, so other indicators are needed to send out quality information, such as friendly, well-informed service staff (see also Chap. 4).

Regarding the different target groups and market segments, it must also be considered that large parts of the demand for cultural tourism have little previous knowledge, a limited time budget and possibly also little leisure time for a more in-depth visit of a cultural heritage site. Here, *edutainment* plays an important role in the conception of services, in which cultural artefacts are made more easily accessible to users (not so much through classical formats like, for example, old-school object signage but rather through digital and "hands on" formats) (DuCros & McKercher, 2020). In this context, it is also important to consider the various *dimensions of the benefits* of cultural tourism services (Coccossis, 2010). In addition to the core benefit, e.g. learning more about a cultural site or object, tourists want to have a good time with their companions (social benefit) and/or show themselves as part of a community of like-minded people (e.g. opera lovers, contemporary art experts) or represent themselves as such (symbolic benefit).

With regard to the selection of concrete instruments within this area of the marketing mix, two findings from the above mentioned Cultural Tourism Study 2018 can be referred to:

- On the one hand, "a lack of strategies (...) [prevents] successful marketing - instead of a focused product policy, cultural tourists are inundated with the same offers over and over again" (Burzinski et al., 2018, p.20; translation by the authors). This will probably also be confirmed by those who take a closer look at the available practical guides. Almost everywhere there is talk of product staging, combination of offers, linking of themes, experience orientation, accessibility, service quality etc.; but if everyone is doing the same (marketing) thing, it is not easy to create sustainable competitive advantages on this basis. At the same time, especially in rural areas, not even certain basic requirements for tourism services are satisfactorily met by cultural and tourism providers. This refers, for example, the guidance systems, the opening hours of the tourist information and/or cultural sites, a clear/structured range of exhibits including modern presentation or staging and object explanation or a modern gastronomic offer.

- On the other hand, as mentioned above, most cultural tourists are not experts in cultural and historical contexts, but rather "flaneurs" who consume culture when travelling besides other things. So when designing cultural tourism services, it is also necessary to think about educational offers that support the reception of the core offer. Here, the use of ICTs (Sect. 2.2.3) and thus the use of contemporary formats/instruments which go beyond traditional guided tours and focus on dialogue and participation, edutainment and the joy of trying new things out is particularly appropriate:

"Apps or mobile websites with similar functions deserve special attention here, as they can be both a marketing and a mediation tool. Thus, a (cultural) tourism app can be not only a service companion, but also a travel and cultural guide. As a permanent companion, it is able to provide the traveller with relevant information and a staged story at any time during the so-called customer journey - from inspiration to arrival to the stay and afterwards. Most destinations have not yet taken up this trend, which manifests itself in a special way in the digital media. However, this could also be due to a lack of financial resources. One thing is certain: There is still a great potential for cooperation here, bringing together mediation and marketing" (Burzinski et al., 2018, p. 65).

3.3 Prices

The pricing policy covers all decisions about the price tourists pay for a particular cultural offer. The price not only influences the decision of cultural tourists to use a service *at all*, but also their *choice* between different offers/competitors. In this context it should be noted that price plays a major role here, especially for commercial service providers, when it comes to managing and stimulating demand. For the public and private non-profit service providers, on the other hand, price plays a much smaller role. Although museums, theatres, etc. should in principle also try to skim off the existing willingness to pay of cultural tourists, nevertheless, admission prices, for example, are usually set under cultural policy aspects (for details see Hausmann, 2019b).

If pricing policy decisions are to be made, the actors in cultural tourism have various strategies at their disposal. These include:

- *Price differentiation*: For what is essentially an identical service (i.e. guided tour of a castle), different prices are charged, taking into account certain criteria.

Suitable criteria in cultural tourism are, for example, *demand-oriented* criteria, such as age (children, senior citizens etc.) or type or status (passionate specialists or casual visitors; group or individual travellers), time aspects, such as e.g. time of use and duration (weekend/during the week, low/main season) or booking/ purchasing date ("early bird" discounts etc.), *quantity-oriented* criteria (e.g. individual or combined services) or *spatial* criteria (e.g. in the centre or outside).

- *Price bundling*: This strategy is often chosen when individual services are complementary and can be bundled into an attractive cultural tourism "package". In this case, guests pay less for the whole package than if they would buy the services individually. In addition, a service package always sends out marketing information (in the sense of: what is available on site, what fits together well) and thus relieves the guest of the burden to decide and organise (Fischbacher & Forster, 2010). Typical examples in cultural tourism are, on the one hand, combined or guest tickets which include admission to either several cultural institutions in the same category (e.g. museum pass) or to various cultural, nature and leisure service providers (e.g. World Heritage Card) and, on the other hand, package tours or weekend offers which include, for example, transport, accommodation, and tickets for cultural events.

With regard to the calculation of the "right" price, i.e. a price that is just about accepted by cultural tourists or that allows for a targeted skimming of the demand-side willingness to pay a price, the methods of (1) *cost-oriented* and (2) *market-oriented* pricing can be distinguished. While the first method is intended to help ensure that all or at least part of a provider's costs are covered by a given price, the latter method can be further broken down into (2a) *demand-oriented* and (2b) *competition-oriented* pricing: While the former method is based on the willingness and acceptance of (potential) cultural tourists to pay prices, the latter examines the prices of competitors and takes them into account in its own pricing. As a rule, it will make sense to *combine* market and cost-oriented considerations in order to set a price that is appropriate from various perspectives: "The final price is ultimately set in the triangle of cost recovery, price sensitivity of the guest and the price level in the destination. The final price must represent good value for money for the guest" (Fischbacher & Forster, 2010).

Effects of Cultural Tourism Cooperation on the Price
Whenever a cultural institution cooperates with a private sector player (e.g. travel agents), a commission must be calculated. If this is not to be passed on to demand, the commission must be earned elsewhere, e.g. through discounted purchasing from suppliers.

3.4   Distribution

Actions in this area of the marketing mix refer to all decisions to be taken in connection with the transfer of the services and products to the demand side. In cultural tourism, too, the concrete selection and design of distribution channels is based on the type of service to be distributed. For example, museums, castles or landscaped gardens, but also, for example, the catering and accommodation industry, require *local* service provision, as their core products (exhibition, accommodation etc.) are highly intangible and as such not tradable. This means that only the *service promise* can be marketed, i.e. the obligation of a cultural tourism service provider to deliver a certain service at an agreed time; this is usually documented using a material medium (admission ticket, booking confirmation etc.). Due to the large interface between distribution and communication measures (Sect. 3.5), which can be easily understood using the example of a website or tourist information, they are often described together in cultural tourism practice (e.g. Burzinski et al., 2018; DTV, 2006; Tourismus NRW, 2019).

As Table 3.1 shows, services or service promises can be distributed in two ways. In *direct* distribution no intermediary is involved between supply and demand, i.e. distribution is handled by the provider himself (at the checkout, on the phone, via his own website etc.). In *indirect* distribution, on the other hand, external bodies are involved, to which the distribution of the promise or touristic service are transferred. Since both distribution channels have advantages and disadvantages, most cultural tourism service providers apply a *multi-channel strategy*.

In addition to the decision areas mentioned, the design of the physical (event) location is also seen as part of the distribution policy. In cultural tourism marketing, the question of how *accessible* and *available* a cultural tourism service is to potential customers must therefore always be answered: "The basis for the integration of cultural offers into the tourism product is availability. In the case of sights, museums etc. this means above all guest-friendly opening hours, at least in the season. What good is the most beautiful village church when it is closed?" (TMB, 2013, p. 27; translation by the authors). Criteria for accessibility are, for example

- Opening or closing times (tourist offices, cultural institutions, restaurants etc.),
- external wayfinding system (signs to the destination and on site),
- internal wayfinding system (signposting at the service provider, such as through a garden/site or in a castle/museum),
- parking spaces (availability, price, signs) or connection to public transport,
- fabric of a building (also and especially in the direct visitor contact area, i.e. entrance/cashier area, sanitary facilities, catering etc.)

Table 3.1 Distribution channels in cultural tourism

	Direct distribution	Indirect distribution
Examples	– Staff (e.g. museum cash desk) – By telephone (e.g. hotel hotline) – Own website / own online booking system	– Tourist-information/presentation – Travel agency/intermediary/organiser – Retail, hotel industry etc. – Ticket portals/ticketing providers
Advantages	– Direct quality control – Own training of the service staff – Direct communication with demand (supports customer orientation, service quality) – No profit sharing or distribution conflicts – Control over prices, advertising etc.	– Extension of the radius, greater target group reach, possibly international focus – Establishing cooperation (possibly useful for other purposes, such as "packaging") – Effectiveness and efficiency advantages through the involvement of a sales specialist (lower costs, no capital commitment, management relief, use of special know-how)
Disadvantages	– Limited radius, small target group, possibly only local/regional focus – Resource-intensive – No efficiency gains – Know-how (e.g. online ticketing) may not be sufficiently available	– Sales commission – No or only indirect quality control – No direct communication with the demand – Common disadvantages of cooperation

- atmosphere (the tourists have a feeling of being welcome at a site) as well as
- educational services (which help to better understand a cultural offer and are thus part of both product and distribution policy).

Visitor Paths as an Important Criterion for Accessibility

At *Salzburg's Mozart museums*, which are highly frequented by tourists, accessibility is guaranteed as in many other "hot spots" as follows: "Sometimes more than 300 people are on the road at the same time. We have therefore timed everything exactly, visitors always walk in one direction only. So there is no oncoming traffic in the narrow corridors, which are barely wider than a person. The entrance runs like a concert. Those who come spontaneously stand in line. Groups that book in advance can enter the museum directly through the 'Fast Lane'" (Laskus, 2018; translation by the authors).

3.5 Communication

The focus of this area of the marketing mix is on the preparation, dissemination and exchange of information between tourism service providers and (potential) customers. On the supplier side, the aim is to attract attention, create knowledge and influence attitudes, expectations and behaviour in the target groups. Communication is either

- *one-stage*, i.e. a cultural tourism service provider sends its messages directly to the recipients (e.g. via direct mail or the website) or
- *multi-stage*, i.e. the provider first addresses its messages to multipliers (city guides, coach tour operators, media, travel bloggers etc.), who in turn pass on the information.

Another distinguishing feature is whether communication is

- *personal*, i.e. there is direct contact between the sender and the recipient (at the box office, reception etc.) or
- *impersonal*, i.e. there is a temporal-spatial separation between the sending of the message (e.g. by e-mail, on flyers and posters) and its reception by the recipient.

All service providers have a wide range of instruments at their disposal that can be used offline or online (for details see Hausmann, 2021; Kotler et al., 2017). The opportunities that the Internet has created for communication policy mean that the individual instruments can also be *networked* with one another ("connectivity"). For example, a classic poster containing a QR code scanned via smartphone/tablet leads to the website or a social media channel. Particularly in urban areas, tourism service providers are increasingly relying on the potential of online communication:

> "Times are changing, requirements are changing: marketing and communication have long been more than just press relations and advertising. Traditional media are losing their importance, but information and inspiration are increasingly sought online. Tourism NRW is therefore increasingly reaching potential guests through new ways and means, from interaction in social networks and blogger relations to its own inspiring website" (Tourismus NRW, 2018, p. 35; translation by the authors).

However, according to the results of the Cultural Tourism Study 2018, in the context of which an online survey with 606 cultural tourism providers was conducted, this claim is less valid for rural areas, where tourism organisations typically do not have the resources to support their local players in such a contemporary way. As Table 3.2 shows, analogue instruments still dominate here (Burzinski et al., 2018).

According to the same study, cultural institutions will also use in particular those instruments that are classics of offline communication (Burzinski et al., 2018, Table 3.3). However, it must be taken into account that the sample includes many institutions from rural areas with few employees and, in some cases, volunteer management (Burzinski et al., 2018); large houses in urban areas are already relying much more frequently on the potential of digital communication.

The interview study by Schuhbauer/Hausmann (2021) shows that things have only changed in parts since then. At least tourism organisations and municipal cultural administrations are becoming more active in the use of ICTs. However, the cultural institutions are still very hesitant in this regard. If at all, they have so far mainly used only already established ICTs, such as social media, for external communication. The following reasons are given by the cultural institutions for this:

Table 3.2 Communication instruments of tourism organisations (multiple answers)

Own brochures on cultural tourism offers	86,3%
Own and/or mediated guided tours to the cultural highlights and special features of the cultural offer	73,2%
Specific cultural tourism thematic area on the website	66,3%
Ticket sales for cultural events within the city/region	64,2%
Current calendar of events differentiated according to target group and cultural interests or branches	60,5%
Development and arrangement of special cultural theme tours and routes as a service for the guest	57,4%
Further information material at the tourist information Centre, e.g. in-depth literature, cultural guides	56,8%
Information on and booking of cultural tourism packages	46,8%
Own cultural event programme, e.g. organisation of an own festival/cultural event	45,8%
Independent websites, microsites, profiles/pages in social media for outstanding or very special cultural offerings	36,3%
Special merchandising products related to the cultural offer	28,4%
An own app with cultural tourism content	17,9%

Source: Burzinski et al., 2018, p. 14; Translation by the authors

Table 3.3 Communication instruments of cultural institutions (multiple answers)

Instruments that tend to be used *frequently*	Instruments that tend *not* to be used *at all*
Press relations (91,7%), Flyers and other print media (98,2%), Events (83,3%) Poster/outdoor advertising (83,3%), Advertisements/supplements in weekly/ monthly magazines (69,2%), Newsletter/E-mail marketing (63,8%), Advertisements/supplements in daily newspapers (63,0%) Trade fair appearances/roadshows (52,9%)	Mobile marketing (80,0%) Guerrilla marketing (77.9%) Blogger relations (73,6%) Advertising on means of transport (62,7%) Guide/sales manual for tour operators/ groups (59,8%) Competitions/contests (54,7%)

Source: Burzinski et al., 2018, p. 36 f.; Translation by the authors

- The lack of staff and financial resources,
- the lack of time,
- non-existent networks or cooperation,
- the frustration from previous projects,
- a general conservative attitude towards digitisation,
- a lack of knowledge about whether the guests use and how they use ICTs,
- the opinion that digital applications are not relevant for a large part of own target groups and
- the opinion that new cultural offerings in general are not necessary.

Recommendations for the implementation and successful use of ICTs
In order to meet the challenges mentioned above, several things therefore need to be taken into account to ensure the implementation and successful use of ICTs. Section 2.2.3 already lists some of these points. However, the authors were able to gain further experience in various interview studies with cultural tourism stakeholders (e.g. Hausmann & Weuster, 2017; Schuhbauer & Hausmann, 2021). These experiences are summarised in Table 3.4 as concrete and practice-related recommendations in the form of questions that cultural tourism actors should ask themselves when implementing and using ICTs.

Table 3.4 Checklist for the implementation and successful use of ICTs

Do we know our target groups and their preferences regarding the use of ICTs? *(see explanations in sect. 2.2.3)*
Do we already use visitor surveys to understand our visitors and learn more about them?
Have we already thought about the advantages we have as an institution through the use of new ICTs? *(possible benefits are e.g.: The networking of different actors; the linking of analogue and digital offerings)*
Are we sufficiently informed about the possible uses and benefits of ICTs? *(keyword: Customer journey, see detailed explanations in sect. 2.2.3)*
Are all the people involved open to the use of ICTs? If not, what doubts remain? Is additional knowledge needed to counter possible prejudices?
What knowledge is already available in our organisation/institution regarding the use of ICTs? And where do we need to catch up?
Which departments within our own institution are already working well together regarding the use of ICTs? And where might there still be a need to catch up?
To what extent do we need new and differently qualified staff to implement digital strategies?
To what extent do we need external support in implementing a digital strategy? *(possible forms of external support are e.g.: Support from (central) tourism organisations or associations for individual cultural institutions; support from the cultural policy level; support within the framework of funding projects)*
What forms of cooperation would make it easier for us to use ICTs in the future? *(see detailed explanations and checklist in section 2.2.4)*
Which ICTs are particularly cost-effective and easy to implement? If we incur long-term costs for the use of a particular ICTs, how can these be covered? *(examples of this are: Payment options; cooperation with other institutions/organisations)*
Have we ever evaluated the success of ICTs we already use? *(possible findings from an evaluation: Whether the right target groups are being addressed; whether the marketing measures taken make sense; how ICTs can be further expanded and established)*
To what extent are there vertical opportunities for interaction at the cultural policy level?
Are there any current funding projects that can support us in implementing digital projects? *(note: Profits can be made here not only from financial support, but also, for example, by acquiring methodological competences or by exchanging ideas with other actors!)*
To what extent are there lessons from other facilities/institutions that we can draw on? *(example: Publicly available information from previous funding projects)*

Implementation decisions: Organisation and People)

4

In parts of the tourism marketing literature, the instrument "people" (personnel policy) is discussed as the fifth "P" (among others Kotler et al., 2017; Meffert et al., 2018). However, the authors understand the service/customer-oriented management of the personnel as an independent field of action at the interface with marketing. Due to the great importance of staff for the production, mediation and marketing of cultural tourism services, the topic is examined in more detail in the following chapter.

People, especially those with direct contact to tourists and also those responsible for the development and marketing of cultural tourism offers, are of great importance for the creation of competitive advantages and visitor benefits – in short: for successful cultural tourism marketing. As pointed out earlier, competitive advantages can be achieved not only through a core service, but also through the "way" in which this service is provided and thus through the competence, friendliness, willingness etc. of the staff (Hausmann, 2021). Therefore, employees are considered the linchpin for success in tourism marketing – and equally so for all providers:

> "Globally, in any particular destination, the tourism industry comprises a range of different-sized public, private and voluntary sector organisations which operate across different elements of tourism supply (accommodation; attractions; food and drink; intermediaries; transport), yet regardless of the nature or size of tourism operations, they are all reliant on the quality of their human resources, i.e. their employees. To achieve competitive advantage in an increasingly competitive market, the success of an individual organization or destination is dependent upon employee contribution and commitment. (...) Employees are the most important assets in a tourism

© The Author(s), under exclusive license to Springer Fachmedien Wiesbaden GmbH, part of Springer Nature 2023
A. Hausmann, S. Schuhbauer, *Basic Guide to Cultural Tourism Marketing*, essentials, https://doi.org/10.1007/978-3-658-39974-0_4

organization and are key to the success of service-sector companies, because of their
critical role in customer interactions" (Haven-Tang & Jones, 2005, p. 90).

In order to use this performance factor as effectively as possible, all cultural
tourism marketing activities must be integrated appropriately into the organisational structure. In the case of larger cultural institutions in urban areas, there will
be a unit – more or less adequately equipped with resources and support – which is
sensibly located in the Communication/PR department and typically pursues cultural tourism marketing "alongside" other marketing tasks. In rural areas with their
small-scale, sometimes even voluntary structure, there will usually not be a sepa-
rate marketing department, often not even a marketing position. Typically, several
functional areas will have to be covered by the same person; often, it will even be
the managers of an institution themselves who try to cover both the strategic and
the operative tasks in cultural tourism marketing. In such cases, it will ultimately
only be possible to successfully develop the market for cultural tourism through the
support of a committed cultural administration which assumes the following tasks:

- The bundling of the various cultural actors under one thematic (local, regional)
  "umbrella",
- preventing parallel structures and offers,
- reduction of rivalries among each other or "church tower thinking", instead ap-
  peal to the joint use of scarce resources,
- fostering cooperation between with local/regional tourism organisations and
  cultural organisations and
- supporting the individual actors by involving (and financing) branding experts,
  establishing an overarching marketing platform etc.

In addition to the (specialist) staff responsible for the development and marketing of cultural tourism offers, numerous other employees at the operational level or
"on the ground" are central to the success of marketing. As outlined in Sect. 3.2,
cultural attractions and heritages – just like any other player in the market (e.g.
tourism organisations, hotels, transport, tour guides) – are service providers, i.e.
they provide services with a high intangible component. Most of the times, cultural
tourists are not able to check the quality of the services offered before using them,
but book them with a more or less high quality risk. In order to counter this risk or
to reduce the quality uncertainty, the staff in service organisations is considered a
decisive factor – in addition to positive "word of mouth" or the recommendation of
trustworthy third parties. Especially the staff at the touchpoints, i.e. where cultural
tourists are in personal, direct contact with a service provider (e.g. telephone, box

office, cloakroom, exhibition rooms), is of considerable importance for overall satisfaction and is used as a *quality surrogate* by demand. The following applies here: The higher the trust characteristics of a service are and the more scarce resources (above all valuable leisure time, but also money etc.) have to be used by tourists, the more important are characteristics of the staff, such as friendliness, advisory competence and service orientation, as well as the ability to remain target group oriented even under stress, as the following example shows.

Stress Management and Storytelling for Successful Services Encounters
When asked what it is like to guide a thousand tourists through Mozart's birthplace every day, a museum educator from the *Salzburg Mozart Museums* in Austria answers:

"Sometimes I get the feeling that they have made an appointment. Then suddenly six or seven groups of visitors stand at the same time in front of the entrance and want to see where Mozart was born. But I don't let myself get stressed, that's the basic requirement for working here. I prefer people who don't just start looking for their wallets at the cash desk, but say directly: two adults, three children, one brochure" (Laskus, 2018; translation by the authors).

Due to her ability to pick up visitors where they stand, the teacher also manages to attract less interested people to Mozart at first:

"Of course, there are also visitors who are bored. They stand in Mozart's kitchen and say: 'Ah, a flat. I like to give them an old coffee roaster from the 18th century. They wonder what that could be. Once they have figured it out, I let them compare their everyday life with Mozart's. Nowadays, I say, you only need two minutes for a cup of coffee. Did you know that Mozart had to wait 45 minutes for his coffee to be ready? People find that incredibly exciting" (Laskus, 2018; translation by the authors).

In this context, it is important to point out the problem that arises from the fact that the service staff, of all people, who are so important for the visitor experience, are often located relatively low down in the hierarchy of cultural attractions and heritage sites, not only organisationally but also "mentally". In the authors experience, this circumstance repeatedly leads to visitor-relevant information being passed on to this group of employees last of all, and it is often not deemed necessary to explain the context for decisions (e.g. postponement of an event programme, lack of online booking facilities) in more detail. Thus, unsatisfactory interactions almost inevitably occur in the exchange between visitors and ticket office staff, for example when a visitor's question is answered: "I don't know that either. That's what we were told to do". This situation is often promoted by the fact that some of the staff are employed by external service providers and may have identity problems with the work. In order to make the situation with the service sector employees successful in view of their great importance for the overall satisfaction of the demanders, it is recommended, among other things to transfer the external marketing with its basic assumptions to the internal organisation. Such "internal marketing" leads to an integrated view of personnel and marketing issues. This has consequences for various areas, namely:

- personnel selection,
- workplace design,
- personnel development and
- a better overall handling of the special working conditions of this group of employees.

Empowerment
One possible concept within "internal marketing" is the concept of "empowerment". It involves delegating responsibility and decision-making authority to lower levels of the hierarchy. The aim here is to expand the scope for action by enabling employees, especially in the service areas with direct contact to tourists and other customers, to largely decide for themselves *how* to carry out a certain task in their area. Instead, the focus is only on the work *result*. For this purpose, the employees are provided with the corresponding resources and competences. Thus, they should not only be able to make decisions independently, but also to solve problems independently (Hausmann, 2021). Example from the museum sector: the box office staff receives complaints, e.g. about inaccessible rooms or about a lent exhibition object being missing. Empowerment enables the box office staff to offer compensation to such tourists (e.g. in the form of a voucher for catering) without having to involve a higher authority in the decision-making process. Service-oriented action in visitor contact can thus take place quickly and unbureaucratically, and tourist satisfaction can be increased on the spot.

Literature

Aaker, D. A. (1996). *Building strong brands*. The Free Press.

Agenzia turistica ticinese SA. (2022). *Bellinzona pass*. https://www.ticino.ch/en/commons/details/Bellinzona-Pass/73499.html. Accessed July 19, 2022.

Bundesministerium für Wirtschaft und Energie (BMWi). (2014). *Tourismusperspektiven im ländlichen Raum. Handlungsempfehlungen zur Förderung des Tourismus in ländlichen Räumen*. https://www.bmwi.de/Redaktion/DE/Publikationen/Tourismus/tourismusperspektiven-in-laendlichen-raeumen.pdf?__blob=publicationFile&v=1. Accessed April 1, 2019.

Burmann, C., Riley, N.-M., Halaszovich, T., & Schade, M. (2017). *Identity-based brand management*. Springer.

Burzinski, M. (2016). Zwischen Herdentrieb und Überwindung der Zwangskooperation. *In Kulturmanagement Magazin, 110*(14–22).

Burzinski, M., Buschmann, L., & Pröbstle, Y. (2018). *Kulturtourismusstudie 2018. Empirische Einblicke in die Praxis von Kultur- und Tourismusakteuren*. https://www.projekt2508.de/wp-content/uploads/2018/05/Kulturtourismusstudie-2018-Webversion.pdf. Accessed December 18, 2018.

Byrnes, W. J. (2009). *Management and the arts* (4th ed.). Elsevier.

Coccossis, H. (2010). Sustainable development and tourism: Opportunities and threats to cultural heritage from tourism. In L. F. Girard & P. Nijkamp (Eds.), *Cultural tourism and sustainable local development* (pp. 47–56). Ashgate.

Deutsche Welle (dw). (2020). *Culture goes digital amid the coronavirus crisis*. https://www.dw.com/en/culture-goes-digital-amid-the-coronavirus-crisis/a-52838447. Accessed: December 16, 2021.

Deutscher Tourismusverband (DTV). (2006). *Städte- und Kulturtourismus in Deutschland*. https://www.deutschertourismusverband.de/service/touristische-studien/dtv-studien.html. Accessed May 26, 2019.

Drda-Kühn, K., & Wiegand, D. (2010). From culture to cultural economic power: rural region development in small German communities. *Creative Industries Journal, 3*(1), 89–97.

DuCros, H., & McKercher, B. (2020). *Cultural tourism* (3rd ed.). Routledge.

Esch, F.-R. (2014). *Strategie und Technik der Markenführung* (8th ed.). Vahlen.

Fischbacher, M./Forster, S. (2010). Erlebnisse und Tourismusangebote schaffen. *Ein Leitfaden für kleinere und mittlere Museen*. : Museen Graubünden.

Föhl, P., & Pröbstle, Y. (2013). Co-operation as a central element of cultural tourism: a German perspective. In M. K. Smith & G. Richards (Eds.), *The routledge handbook of cultural tourism* (pp. 75–83). Routledge.

Haus der Geschichte der Bundesrepublik Deutschland Foundation. (2022). *Organigramm der Stiftung Haus der Geschichte der Bundesrepublik Deutschland*. https://www.hdg.de/fileadmin/bilder/07-Stiftung/Organisation/Organigramm_01072022.pdf. Accessed July 19, 2022.

Hausmann, A. (2018). *Digitale Angebote im Kulturtourismus. Zur Nutzung von Kommunikations- und Informationstechnologien (IKT). Ergebnisse einer Besucherbefragung beim UNESCO-Welterbe Zollverein*. https://kulturmanagement.ph-ludwigsburg.de/fileadmin/subsites/2c-kuma-t-01/PDF/Forschung/Forschungsbericht_Digitale_Angebote_im_Kulturtourismus.pdf. Accessed May 5, 2019.

Hausmann, A. (2019a). *Einführung in den Kulturtourismus. Praxis Kulturmanagement*. Springer Gabler.

Hausmann, A. (2019b). *Kompaktwissen Kulturmanagement. Reihe Kunst- und Kulturmanagement* (2nd ed.). Springer.

Hausmann, A. (2021). *Kulturmarketing, series Arts and culture management* (3rd ed.). Springer.

Hausmann, A., & Schuhbauer, S. (2020). The role of information and communication technologies in cultural tourist's journeys: the case of a World Heritage Site. *Journal of Heritage Tourism, 16*(6), 669–683.

Hausmann, A., & Weuster, L. (2017). Possible marketing tools for heritage tourism: the potential of implementing information and communication technology. *Journal of Heritage Tourism, 13*(3), 273–284.

Haven-Tang, C., & Jones, E. (2005). Human resource management in tourism businesses. In J. Beech & S. Chadwick (Eds.), *The business of tourism management* (pp. 89–113). Pearson Education.

Homburg, C. (2017). *Grundlagen des Marketingmanagement* (5th ed.). Gabler.

Interreg Europe. (2021). *Good practice: Riberana – online experiences to visit natural routes and museums*. https://www.interregeurope.eu/policylearning/good-practices/item/3905/riberana-online-experiences-to-visit-natural-routes-and-museums/. Accessed December 16, 2021.

Keller, K. L. (1993). Conceptualizing, Measuring and Managing Customer-Based Brand Equity. *In Journal of Marketing, 57*(1), 1–22.

Kohlen, C. (2017). Vom Mahner zum Motivator. Besucherorientierung von Service- und Aufsichtskräften. In O. Scheytt & F. Loock (Eds.), *Handbuch Kulturmanagement, E 3.15* (pp. 97–120). Raabe.

Kolb, B. (2017). *Tourism marketing for cities and towns: Using branding and events to attract tourists* (2nd ed.). Routledge.

Kotler, P./Bowen, J.T./Makens, J.C./Baloglu, S. (2017). Marketing for Hospitality and Tourism 5th Prentice Hall.

Kozak, M./Baloglu, S. (2011). Managing and marketing tourist destinations. Routledge: .

Laskus, M. (2018). *Wie es wirklich ist...täglich tausend Touristen durch Mozarts Geburtshaus zu führen.* https://www.zeit.de/2018/30/museumspaedagogin-salzburg-mozarttourismus. Accessed May 20, 2019.

Law, R./Buhalis, D./Cobanoglu, C. (2014). Progress on information and communication technologies in hospitality and tourism. *International Journal of Contemporary Hospitality Management*, 26(5), 727–750.

Meffert, H., Bruhn, M., & Hadwich, K. (2018). *Dienstleistungsmarketing* (9th ed.). Gabler.

Mendonca, V. J. D., Cunha, C. R., & Morais, E. P. (2018). The potential of cooperative networks to leverage tourism in rural regions. Paper presented at the 13th Iberian Conference on Information systems and Technologies (CISTI), available at: https://ieeexplore. ieee.org/document/8399288. Accessed August 13, 2020.

Museo Galileo. (2018). *App and printable Mini-Guides. Museo Galileo App.* https://www. museogalileo.it/en/museum/visit/app-and-printable-miniguides.html. Accessed December 16, 2021.

Neumeier, S., & Pollermann, K. (2014). Rural Tourism as Promoter of Rural Development – prospects and limitations: case study findings from a pilot project promoting village tourism. *European Countryside, 6*(4), 270–296.

Polese, F. (2010). Local government and networking trends supporting sustainable tourism: Some empirical evidence. In L. F. Girard & P. Nijkamp (Eds.), *Cultural tourism and sustainable local development* (pp. 131–148). Ashgate.

Polo, A.I./Frias, D. (2010). Collective Strategies for Rural Tourism: the experience of networks in Spain. *Journal of Tourism Consumption and Practice*, 2(1), 25–45.

Promote Iceland. (2017). Target groups. *For Icelandic Tourism.* https://www.islandsstofa.is/ media/1/targetgroups-iceland.pdf. Accessed December 2, 2021.

Raich, F., & Zehrer, A. (2013). Einfluss der Besonderheiten und Ausprägungen touristischer Netzwerke auf die Produktentwicklung. *tw Zeitschrift für Tourismuswissenschaft, 5*(1), 5–21.

Schlösserland Sachsen. (2019). *Marketingverbund Schlösserland Sachsen.* www. schloesserland-sachsen.de/de/marketingverbund-schloesserland-sachsen/. Accessed April 20, 2019.

Schuhbauer, S., & Hausmann, A. (2021). Cooperation for the implementation of digital. applications in rural cultural tourism marketing. *International Journal of Culture, Tourism and Hospitality Research, 16*(1), 106–120.

Schuhbauer, S., & Hausmann, A. (2022). Der touristische Einsatz von Informations- und Kommunikationstechnologien in Kultureinrichtungen im ländlichen Raum: Eine interviewbasierte ressourcentheoretische Untersuchung. *Zeitschrift für Tourismuswissenschaft, 14*(2), 134–163.

Staatliche Kunstsammlungen Dresden (SKD). (2019). *Diversity in unity: The new corporate design of the Staatliche Kunstsammlungen Dresden.* https://www.skd.museum/en/about-us/corporate-design/. Accessed April 6, 2019.

Städel Museum. (2021). *The Städel Museum's digital offers.* https://www.staedelmuseum. de/en/digital-offers. Accessed December 16, 2021.

Theaterhaus Stuttgart. (2021). *DanceAR: Augmented reality app.* https://www.theaterhaus. com/theaterhaus/index.php?id=1,2,883. Accessed December 16, 2021.

Tourism NRW e.V. (2018). *Jahresbericht.* https://www.touristiker-nrw.de/wp-content/uploads/2018/03/Webversion-des-Jahresberichts-2017.pdf. Accessed January 6, 2019.

Tourism NRW e.V. (2019). *Marketingmaßnahmen 2019.* https://www.touristiker-nrw.de/wp-content/uploads/2019/02/Tourismus-NRW-Marketingplan_2019.pdf. Accessed April 3, 2019.

Tourismus Brandenburg (TMB). (2013). *Kulturtourismus in Brandenburg.* https://mwfk. brandenburg.de/media_fast/4055/Leitfaden_Kulturtourismus.15995197.pdf. Accessed April 6, 2019.

Tourismus Marketing GmbH Baden-Württemberg (TMBW). (2011). *Strategische Marketingkonzeption Tourismus Marketing GmbH Baden-Württemberg.* https://www.tourismus-bw.de/Media/B2B/Tourismus-Marketing-GmbH-Baden-Wuerttemberg. Accessed April 4, 2019.

Van der Zee, E., & Vanneste, D. (2015). Postprint version of article Tourism networks unravelled; a review on the literature on networks in tourism management studies. *Tourism Management Perspective, 15,* 46–56.

Visit Estonia. (2020). *Experience-led travel. Visit Estonia. Brand Strategy and Story.* https:// brand.estonia.ee/wp-content/uploads/2020/12/VisitEstonia_Brand_Strategy_Story.pdf. Accessed December 3, 2021.

VisitBritain/Visit England. (2021a). *Who we are & what we do.* https://www.visitbritain.org/ who-we-are-what-we-do. Accessed December 3, 2021.

VisitBritain/Visit England. (2021b). *Our five year strategy.* https://www.visitbritain.org/our-five-year-strategy. Accessed December 3, 2021.

West, D. C., Ford, J. B., & Ibrahim, E. (2015). *Strategic marketing. Creating competitive advantage* (3rd ed.). Oxford University Press.

World Tourism Organization (UNWTO). (2019a). *High-level dialogue on digital skills in tourism.* http://europe.unwto.org/event/high-level-dialogue-digital-skills-tourism. Accessed May 20, 2019.

World Tourism Organization (UNWTO). (2019b). *UNWTO Guidelines for Institutional Strengthening of Destination Management Organizations (DMOs).* https://www.e-unwto.org/doi/pdf/10.18111/9789284420841. Accessed January 2, 2021.

Württemberg State Museum. (2022). *Mitarbeiter*innen des Landesmuseums Württemberg.* https://www.landesmuseum-stuttgart.de/museum/team. Accessed July 19, 2022.

Yu Park, H. (2014). *Heritage tourism.* Routledge.